REALLY, REALLY BIG QUESTIONS about Me and My Body

KINGFISHER
NEW YORK

www.tthp.org

Published in the United States by Kingfisher,
175 Fifth Ave., New York, NY 10010
Kingfisher is an imprint of Macmillan Children's Books, London.

Distributed in the U.S. and Canada by Macmillan, 175 Fifth Ave., New York, NY 10010

Library of Congress Cataloging-in-Publication data has been applied for.

Consultant: Holly Cave

ISBN: 978-0-7534-6892-0

Printed in China
1 3 5 7 9 8 6 4 2
1TR/0712/UTD/WKT/140WF

Picture credit: Fibonacci/Wikipedia p.24

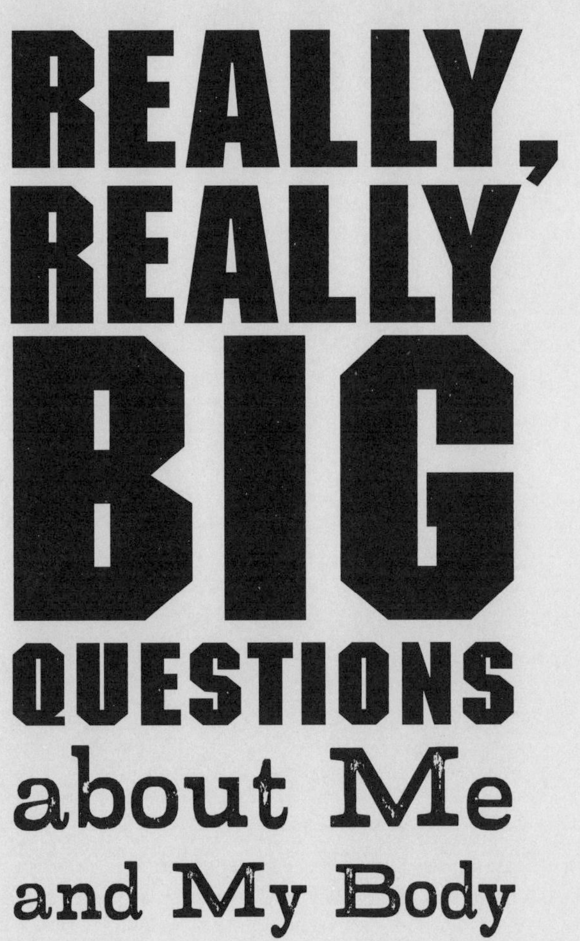

REALLY, REALLY BIG QUESTIONS about Me and My Body

Dr. Stephen Law

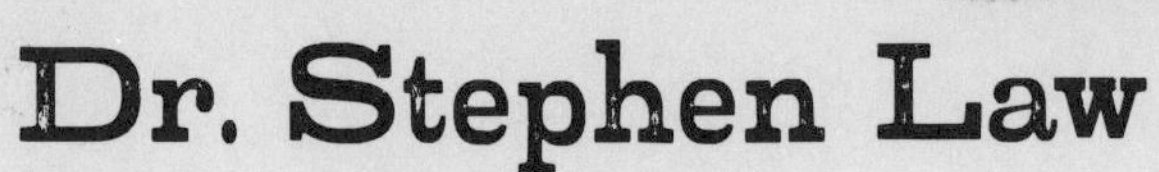

illustrated by

Marc Aspinall

CONTENTS

CHAPTER 1
WHO AM I?

CHAPTER 2
HOW DOES MY BODY WORK?

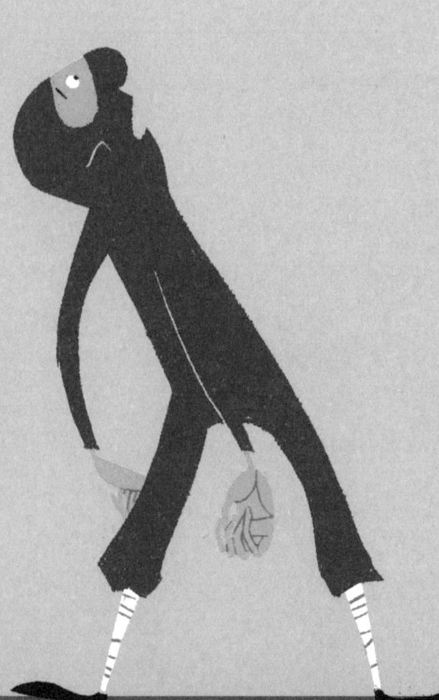

CHAPTER 3
MIND-BOGGLING ME

CHAPTER 4
WHAT CAN I KNOW?

INTRODUCTION

WHO ARE YOU?

DR. STEPHEN LAW

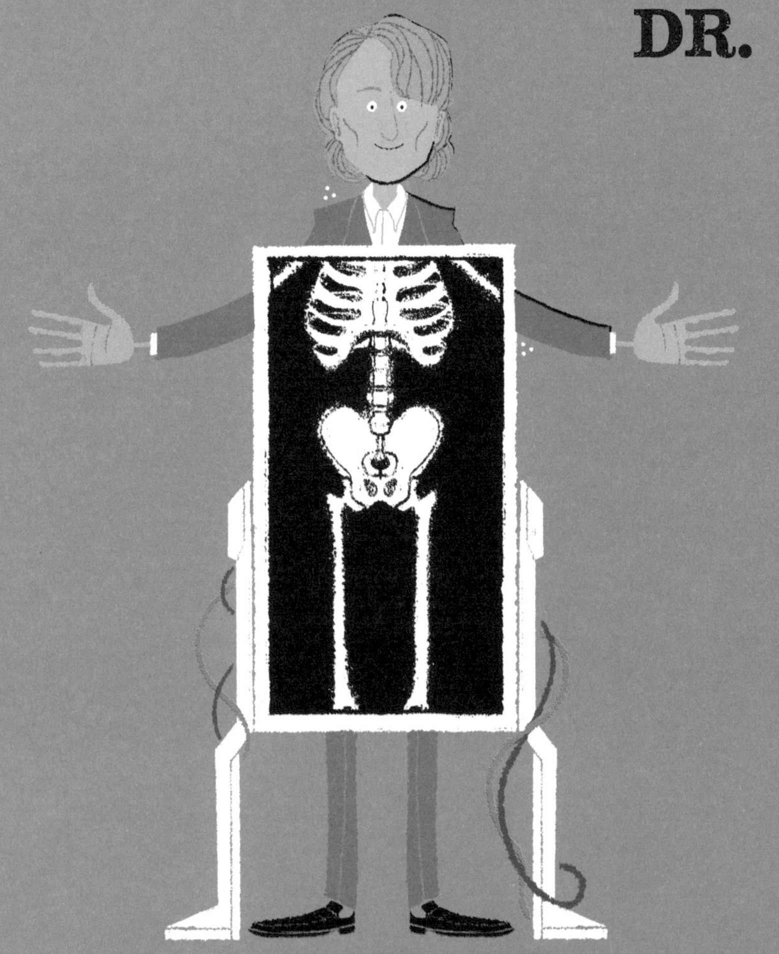

You are a human being—one of the wonders of the universe.

In this unimaginably huge universe, the only life that we know about is on this tiny planet. Here we are, drifting through space on a ball of rock that goes around a star every year. That star is just one of hundreds of billions in our galaxy, and our galaxy is just *one* of more than a hundred billion galaxies in the universe.

Life began here between 3.6 and 3.8 billion years ago. However, human beings have been around for only about 200,000 years. All sorts of extraordinary animals existed before we showed up—including the dinosaurs, which died out about 65 million years ago.

For most of the time that humans have lived on Earth, life was simple. People were part of small groups. They made rough shelters from the materials around them. There was no money. There were no cities or roads. There was no farming, either. Food had to be hunted or gathered from wherever it could be found.

Farming, roads, and cities first appeared just a few thousand years ago. Modern science really only appeared a few hundred years ago. In a very short time, we have utterly transformed planet Earth—and ourselves.

Among all the different forms of life on this planet, we are the first to: begin to understand where we came from; begin to understand how both we, and our planet, were formed; appreciate the huge scale of the universe; and grapple with some *immense* questions about ourselves, such as:

Why am I here?
Where did I come from?
How do I see?
What am I made of?
How do I know that I am real?
Why do I feel pain?

This is a book bursting with really, really big questions . . . about *you*!

Are you ready to blow your mind?

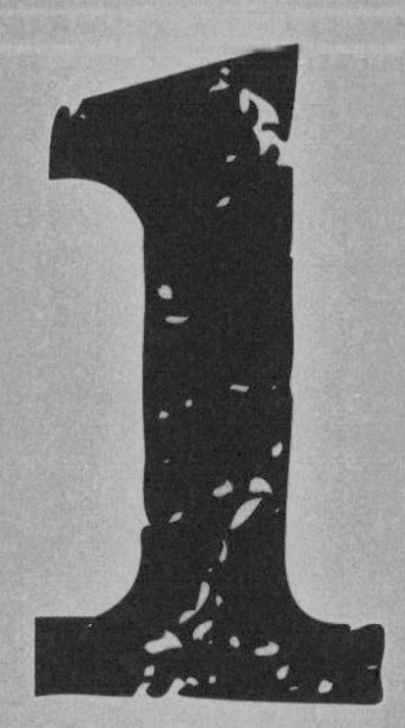

WHO AM I?

Where did you come from? Where did any of us come from? All around the world, different cultures have created their own stories and myths to answer these questions. For example, the ancient Norse people believed the first humans were made from tree trunks. Let's find out what scientists have discovered.

Also, let's think about what makes you *you*. If we changed your hair color or the shape of your nose, it would still be you. But what if we gave you a new body or completely different memories? Would that still be you? Let's see if we can figure out the answers to these questions.

WHERE DID I COME FROM?

You are a human being, and human beings always come from a mother and a father.

It all begins with an egg from the mother and a sperm cell from the father that goes into the egg to fertilize it. The egg cell then divides to make two cells, those two cells then each divide to make four cells, and so on.

Gradually, these cells form an embryo that, over time, grows into a fetus. Finally, after about nine months, the mother gives birth. Out comes a new human.

Usually, all of this takes place in the mother's womb. However, modern science and technology mean that things have changed. Today, some children are grown from an egg taken from one woman, but fertilized in a science laboratory and then grown inside the womb of another, different woman.

Not everyone ends up with their "biological" mother and father—the male and female who provided the sperm and the egg. Some of us end up with new parents who love and raise us just like any other mom or dad.

WHERE DID WE ALL COME FROM?

You came from a "biological" mother and father. But where did they come from? Of course, they had their own parents, who also had parents. But where did the very first human parents come from?

Almost all scientists believe that the first modern humans appeared around 200,000 years ago. We evolved gradually from an earlier humanlike species, which in turn evolved from an earlier species.

In fact, most scientists today believe that every living thing on this planet is related. Your family tree goes right back to the first tiny, simple living things that appeared on Earth around 3.7 billion years ago.

So, every living thing on this planet is one of your very, very distant relatives. Even that snail and that flower!

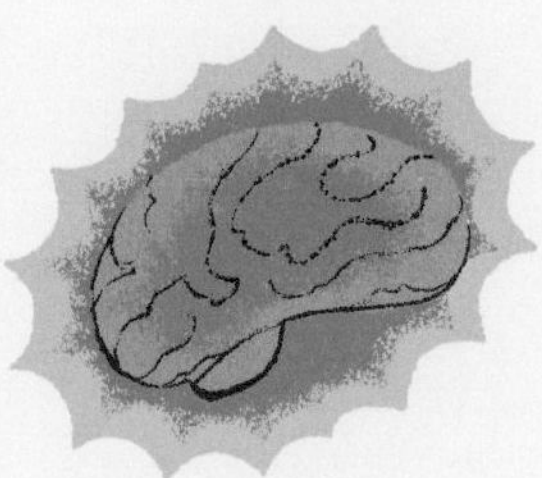

BRAIN BURN!

Living things can gradually evolve into new life forms. But how did the first living things appear?

WHAT AM I HERE FOR?

This is a difficult question to answer. Each generation of living creatures is made to reproduce. So, in a way, your purpose is to reproduce—to have your own children.

However, although that may be what nature has made you for, you don't have to reproduce. That's up to you. You can make your own decisions about how to live your life. You can decide whether to have children. You can decide whether to learn to play a musical instrument and what kind of job you want to have. Some choices we make are important; others are less so. You could even try to become the world hot-dog-eating champion.

IF I CHANGE, AM I STILL ME?

Humans change. We grow bigger, for example.

Our minds change, too, of course—you don't always feel the same way every day. Some days we are happier, others we are grumpier. Our memories change as well. Every day, we have new experiences to remember.

You are changing all the time. Yet when we look at a photo album with pictures of you as a tiny baby, then a toddler, then walking and talking, it's always *you* that we see, isn't it? So what *makes* it you?

Maybe it's the fact that it's the same living body that we see in each picture that makes them you? Your body may have changed in many ways—such as its size and shape—but it's still the same living thing.

So perhaps *you are your body*. You end up wherever your body ends up, even if it does change a lot during your lifetime.

COULD I SWAP BODIES WITH SOMEONE ELSE?

If you are your body, then it seems that you are stuck with the same body for your entire life. But are you?

Ben and Jack have taken a field trip to a science lab, where Professor Clunk has created an extraordinary machine. She calls it the *Mind-move-a-tron*.

Professor Clunk demonstrates the machine by placing the helmets on Ben and Jack's heads. The computer scans Ben and Jack's brains and records exactly how they are put together. Then, in a flash, it reorganizes Jack's brain so that it is like Ben's was and Ben's brain so that it is like Jack's was.

Then the Professor asks the person sitting in Ben's chair his name. Because his brain is just like Jack's, it now stores all of Jack's memories. So, although he has Ben's body, he says, "My name is Jack." When he looks in the mirror, he is amazed. He remembers having Jack's face, yet now he sees Ben's face looking back at him.

Of course, the person with Jack's body now *thinks* he is Ben.

So who now has Ben's body? Ben or Jack? It's a tricky question, but the answer seems to be: Jack. It seems as if Ben and Jack have *swapped bodies*!

Of course, this is just a story, and no such machine has been invented. But perhaps it will be built one day. If so, then it seems people *could* swap bodies.

IS MY MEMORY WHAT MAKES ME *ME*?

So what makes someone Jack, if it's not that they have Jack's body?

Perhaps the answer is—having Jack's *memories*. The reason that it's Jack in Ben's body is that that's where Jack's memories ended up. By rearranging the two brains, Professor Clunk's machine switched around Ben and Jack's memories. That switched around Ben and Jack.

They ended up where their memories ended up.

So perhaps you end up wherever your memories end up. Perhaps it's your memory that makes you *you*. What do you think?

"Memory . . . is the diary that we all carry about with us."

Miss Prism
From *The Importance of Being Earnest* (1895)
by Oscar Wilde

WHEN I'M EIGHTY, WILL I STILL BE THE SAME PERSON?

Philosopher John Locke, who lived more than 300 years ago, believed that it *is* your memory that makes you *you*.

But it seems that Locke's theory isn't exactly right. Locke thought that you are the same person as an earlier person *only* if you remember being that earlier person. So what happens if you lose your memories?

I can't remember anything from when I was a young child. Not a thing. There's a photo of me riding a pony when I was two, but I can't remember riding the pony. So Locke's theory says I am not that small child in the photo. But I am!

Maybe we can fix Locke's theory so that I can still be the same person as the child in the photo.

Perhaps to be that two-year-old, I don't have to remember all the way back to when I was that person. I can't remember when I was two, but I can remember when I was ten. And when I was ten I could remember when I was five. And when I was five, I could remember when I was three, and when I was three I could remember when I was two. So although I can't now remember all the way back to when I was two, my memories still link me back to that person in the photo. Maybe *that's* why he and I are the same person.

If so, then even when I am 80, I can still be the same person as that child in the photo. Even if I can't remember when I was young, my memories still link me back to that time.

COULD THERE BE MORE THAN ONE OF ME?

Professor Clunk's *Mind-move-a-tron* machine seemed to swap Ben and Jack's minds around, but *maybe* people don't have to end up where their memories end up.

Suppose Professor Clunk builds another, even more extraordinary machine, called the *Replicator*.

Two boxes are connected by wires to a computer. Jack stands in the first box, and his entire body is scanned. Then *fzzzt*!—there's a flash. His body is instantly and painlessly destroyed, but a new body exactly like his old one is created in the second box. This new body has a brain just like his old brain and memories identical to his old memories. This new body looks just like Jack. If we ask this person who they are, they'll say, "Jack." They *think* they are *Jack*.

But are they?

If people end up where their memories end up, it seems that the person who steps out of the other box really is Jack. This machine destroys one body in one box and makes a copy of it in the other—it moves the person from one box to the other.

However, Professor Clunk then adjusts her new machine. Now the machine doesn't destroy the first body. Instead it makes a new body in the second box, but the first body is still around.

There are now two people that look just like Jack. In fact, both think they are Jack. But which, if either of them, *really is Jack*?

What do you think?

If people end up wherever their memories end up, then it seems that both of these people are Jack. But they can't be the same person, as there are two of them, not one. They are exactly alike, of course, but they aren't one and the same person.

So, if they aren't both Jack, then it seems that people don't necessarily end up where their memories end up! At least one of them has Jack's memories, but isn't Jack!

Then which one is Jack, if either? And why? This is a tricky puzzle—a puzzle that philosophers are still struggling with. You may have your own ideas . . .

IS THERE LIFE

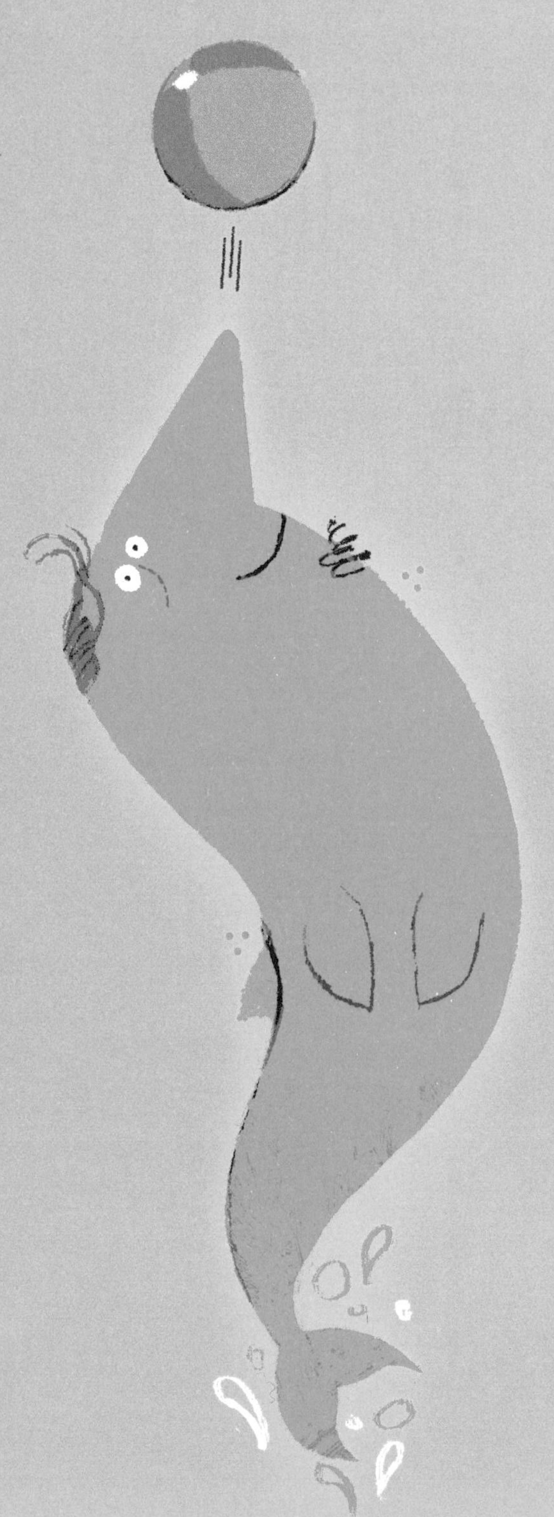

Human beings are a type of animal. When other animals die—a shrimp, a cow, or a monkey, for example—many of us suppose that that's the end of them. But are humans different?

Some people think that when a human body dies, the person can still continue—they believe that you have a *soul*.

Many people believe that your soul is something connected to, but separate from, your physical body. It's something that can survive without any human body at all. It can float off and exist on its own. Some people believe that after we die, our souls may go to a wonderful place that they call heaven.

Others believe that people—and animals—are reincarnated. They think that, after we die, we may be reborn. In fact, some suppose that we may be reborn again and again, and perhaps not as a human. In a previous life you might have been a mosquito, a dolphin, or even a king.

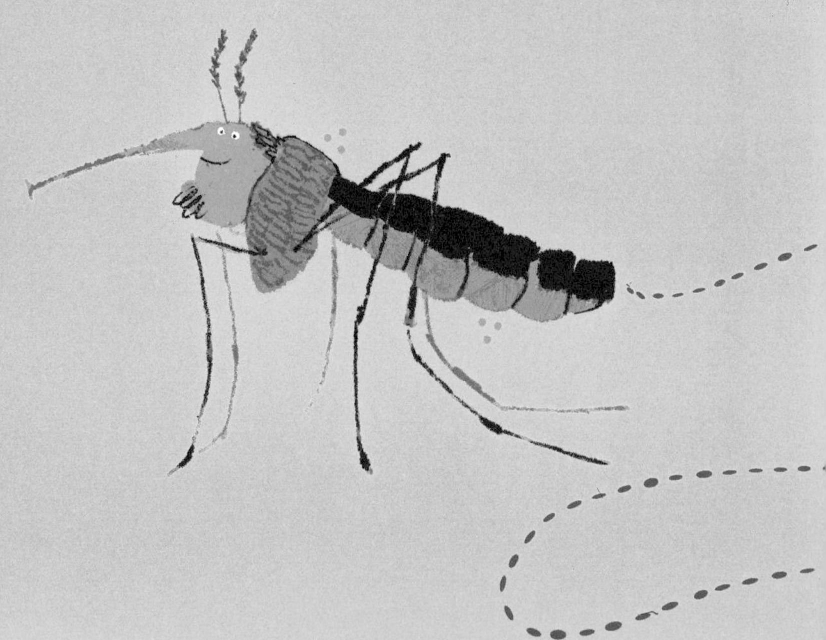

AFTER DEATH?

Perhaps we cannot know, absolutely and for sure, what happens to us when we die. But, if this might be the only life we have, it seems sensible to try to make the most of it. We should try to get as much out of our lives as we can—by enjoying our lives and by trying to help others enjoy theirs, too.

Perhaps one day, technology will let us live longer than our bodies. Perhaps scientists will be able to create new, young bodies for us as we grow old, and then use a *Mind-move-a-tron* machine to move us into these new, young bodies. Then people could live for a very long time, long after their original bodies had died.

But does the *Mind-move-a-tron really* move people from one body to another? I'm not sure! What do you think?

BRAIN BURN!

If humans have an afterlife, what is it like? What do we do there? Can we get bored? Can we misbehave? If not, why not?

HOW DOES MY BODY WORK?

You are a human being—a type of animal. But what is an animal? Of course we know that ducks, whales, slugs, fish, and ants are all animals. And flowers, trees, mushrooms, and bacteria aren't. But what's the difference?

One important feature of animals is that they can move themselves around. You can go for a walk; mushrooms can't.

Another difference is that most animals have digestive pathways. Food goes in one end, and waste comes out the other. And the food of an animal is other living things, such as plants and other animals. Most plants don't eat other living things (though some do, such as the Venus flytrap, which traps and eats flies).

You have a stomach and intestines in which you can digest a burger. Flowers and trees don't have anything like that.

Let's find out more about this body of yours. How does it work? Why does it grow? Why does it get sick? And how do medicines make it better?

WHAT AM I MADE OF?

Your body is made out of tiny living parts called *cells*. Cells are said to be "the building blocks of life." All living things are made out of cells, whether it's only one cell, like some bacteria; a thousand cells, like a roundworm; or trillions of cells, like tigers or trees.

The simplest living things on this planet are single-celled creatures, such as bacteria.

Bacteria are tiny organisms that can be found almost everywhere on the planet. Look at your hands. They are covered with millions of bacteria right now! You can't see them because they are very small—far too small to see without the help of a microscope.

Of course, your body isn't a single cell. Just like all other animals and plants, you are made out of many different types of cells. In fact, a human body is made up of about one hundred trillion cells—including skin cells, brain cells, and hundreds of other kinds of cells.

So your body is *made out of cells*—and these cells are made up of *atoms* that come together in groups to form *molecules*. Still with me?

Atoms are *incredibly* small. If an atom were 3 ft. (1m) high, you would be 6 million miles (10 million km) tall!

There are many different kinds of atoms in your body. They include atoms from substances such as *calcium, carbon, hydrogen, iron, nitrogen, oxygen, phosphorus,* and *sulfur*. These substances, made up of just one type of atom, are called elements. Almost all of these elements *were made inside stars that exploded billions of years ago.*

So you are made out of *cells*. You are made out of *atoms* and *molecules*. And you are also made out of *stardust*!

WHAT'S LIVING INSIDE ME?

More than you might think! Like all human beings, you are made out of cells. But here's a creepy fact. A big amount of the cells in your body *aren't yours*! In fact, they *aren't even human*!

So whose cells *are* they then? Well, most of the cells in your body belong to single-celled creatures—mainly different kinds of bacteria. Weirdly, your body contains about *ten times* as many bacterial cells as it does human cells! If you were to suck out all of the bacterial cells from your body they would fill a 4 pt. (2L) jug.

Perhaps you think that sounds like a *bad* thing?

It's true that some bacteria are harmful, but actually, only a tiny fraction of bacteria do us harm. Some are actually *good* for us. They can do things like help you digest food. In fact, without all those bacteria living inside you, you would be a lot less healthy. Those bacteria are your friends!

HOW DO I SEE?

Like many living things, you have eyes that allow you to see.

So how do your eyes work? Well, we all know that when it's dark, we humans can't see very much. We need light to see. Light hits the objects around us, and some of it bounces off and passes through the thin film covering the eye and into the black hole in the middle of each eye—the *pupil*.

There's also a *lens* in each eye, behind the pupil. This lens focuses the light coming in to produce an upside-down image at the back of the eye.

The back of the eye is a screen, called the *retina*, which is made up of millions of special cells. These cells are sensitive to light. When light falls on one of these cells, it sends out a little electrical charge. The patterns of electrical charge sent by all the cells on the retina are sent to a nerve, called the *optic nerve*, at the back of the eye. The two optic nerves—one from each eye—connect to your brain. At the back of the brain, the *visual cortex* then gets to work on the electrical signals received.

The brain then has a *lot* of work to do to allow you to see correctly. One thing the brain does is turn the upside-down image the right way up again.

Another thing that your brain does is to *fill in the gaps in what you see*. One very strange gap is called the *blind spot*. It lies at the place where the optic nerve leaves the back of your eye. There are no light-sensitive cells there. So no image is sent to the brain from that part of your retina. You're actually blind at that spot. But you aren't aware of your blind spot, are you?

You can prove that you have a blind spot by trying this experiment. Close your right eye and bring this book close to your face (about two finger lengths away should do it). Look with your left eye at the **X** below. Can you see the **O** over to the left? You should be able to.

Now *slowly* pull the book away from your face. What happens when the book is about 10 in. (25cm) away? The O disappears! Pull the book a bit farther away and it will reappear!

The O disappears because the image passes across your blind spot. You don't normally notice that you are blind right there, because *your brain fills in the gap for you*!

How much of what you seem to see is really there and how much is added by your brain, do you think? Is a tomato really red? Or does color exist only in our minds? Do you see the same colors as your best friend?

This famous illusion also illustrates how our brains can create things that are not really there.

You can probably "see" a white triangle hovering over these black shapes. Yet there is no triangle there!

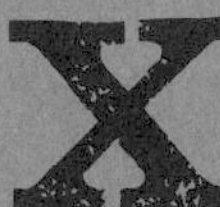

HOW DO I MOVE MY BODY?

When you decide to turn this page, out goes your arm and then your fingers flip the paper over. But *how* are you able to do this?

Wiggle your fingers. Your fingers are being moved by muscles, which are joined to your bones by cords called tendons. You can probably see the tendons moving on the back of your hand when you wiggle your fingers.

But what's making the muscles in your arm and fingers move? Electricity—believe it or not! Tiny electrical signals are being sent from your brain down through your spinal cord and a pathway of cells called *nerves* that link your muscles to your brain. These electrical signals cause your muscles to contract, and that makes your fingers wiggle. This is also how you are able to move other parts of your body such as your legs.

The first step to discovering that *electricity* makes our muscles move was taken a long time ago—back in 1791, by Luigi Galvani. He found that the muscles of dead frogs twitched when an electric spark struck them.

In fact, sometimes people become sick because the tiny electrical signals that make their heart beat are too weak or at the wrong speed to make their heart (a muscle) work correctly. So some people are fitted with a device in their chest called a pacemaker. It gives their heart a small jolt of electricity when it's needed.

But beware. A big shock of electricity can stop your heart from beating forever. *Electricity is dangerous stuff.*

"Look! It's moving. It's alive."

From the movie *Frankenstein* (1931)

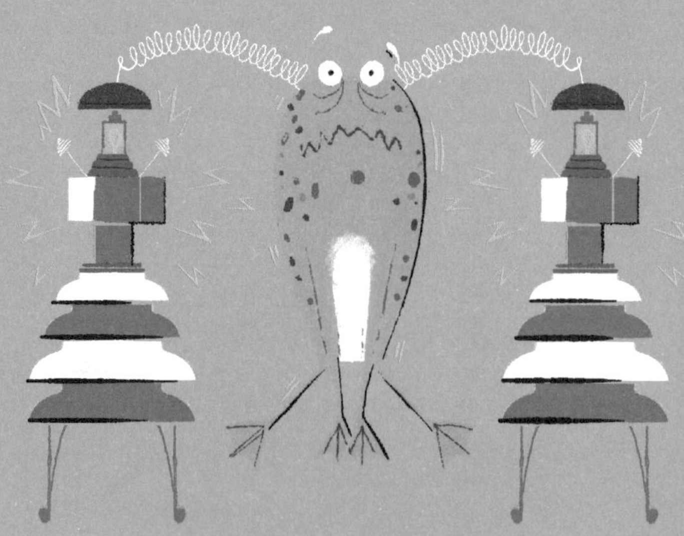

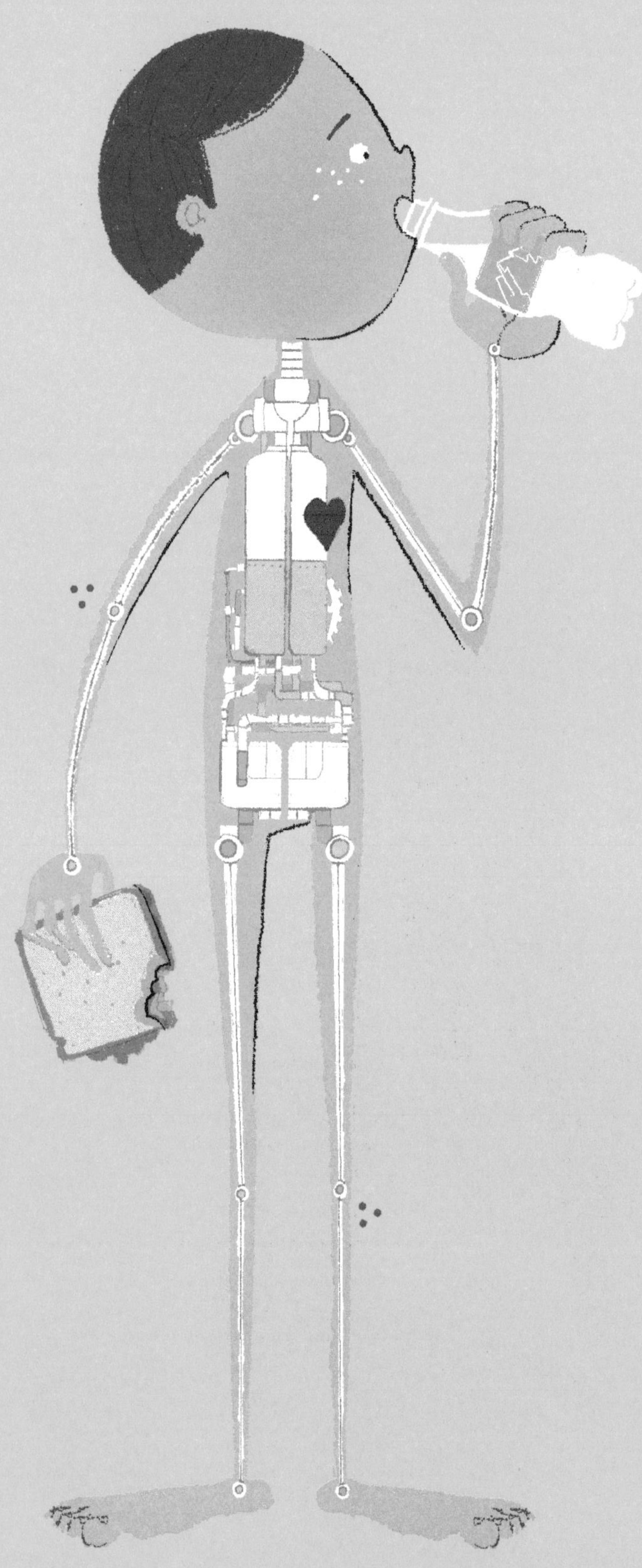

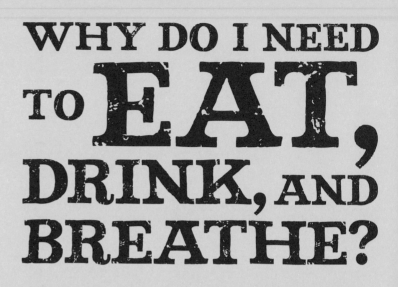

WHY DO I NEED TO EAT, DRINK, AND BREATHE?

Your body needs food, air, and water to survive. That's because, in order to continue working properly, the cells in your body need certain things. They need *oxygen* (which comes from the air that you breathe) and *water*. They also need *energy* and other substances to keep going.

So how do the trillions of cells that make up your body get what they need?

When you eat and drink, food and water go in through your mouth and down a tube into your stomach. When you breathe, air goes in through your mouth and nose and down a different tube into your lungs. As blood is pumped around your body by your heart, the blood goes to your lungs to collect the oxygen taken from the air. Nutrients from food are also passed into your blood. The nutrients and oxygen are then pumped around your body, in your blood, to the cells that need them.

Just like a car that doesn't get water, air, and gasoline put into it, your body will break down if it doesn't get supplied with water, air, and food.

So how long can you go without a refill?

- Without *oxygen*, you'll probably die within three to five minutes.
- Without *water*, you'll die within a few days, maybe less if you are in a dry, hot place.
- Without *food* you can actually survive for a few weeks.

WHY DO I LOVE CHOCOLATE?

Most humans love fatty, sweet foods like chocolate. But *why* do we love them *so* much?

The explanation lies way back in our history. Thousands of years ago, before farming was invented, humans needed to hunt and gather food.

Back then, sweet and fatty foods were difficult to find. But they were very valuable to our ancestors, as they are packed full of energy. When food is scarce, finding foods with a lot of fat and sugar helps you survive.

Now, humans that weren't excited about sweet and fatty foods would have been less likely to find and eat them. So they would have been *less* likely to survive and have children. Those born with a liking for fat and sugar would probably have eaten more of them and been *more* likely to survive and have children. If a liking for this type of food is passed on to their children, then the human race as a whole will gradually come to really like sweet and fatty foods.

So that's one of the main reasons you love chocolate!

But here's the problem. All those thousands of years ago, it was difficult to find and eat too much sweet and fatty foods. Now it's easy. Stores provide us with an endless supply of them. We can eat as much as we want. But that's *way too much*! Our bodies can't take it. Eat loads of sugar and fat and your teeth will rot, you'll get really fat, and your body will become more and more unhealthy.

WHY DO I GROW?

Children, like you, grow because of things called *hormones*. There's a growth hormone that's made by a gland in your brain. The hormone is a substance that goes into your bloodstream and gets pumped around your body, where, among other things, it makes cells start to divide. That makes you get bigger.

Babies grow very quickly—about 10 in. (25cm) in their first year. After the age of two, children grow about 2 in. (6cm) per year until they are between the ages of 8 and 13, when they have another growth spurt.

Our bodies can grow in other ways, too. One way that you can make parts of your body grow bigger—your muscles—is by using them a lot. Some people go to the gym and lift weights. That can really make your muscles grow bigger. Bodybuilders change their bodies in amazing ways by weightlifting. They grow *huge* muscles, which they show off in bodybuilding competitions.

Bodybuilders have to keep lifting weights to keep the big muscles they have grown. Once they stop, their muscles soon shrink back to their normal size.

WHY CAN I GROW NEW TOENAILS, BUT NOT A NEW LEG?

Every few weeks, you have to cut your toenails and fingernails. They just keep on growing. Recently a friend of mine lost his entire big toenail. But a new toenail grew back. If you shave off your hair, it soon grows back, too.

So *some* parts of our bodies grow back when they get cut off. But not many do—and definitely not your legs!

But that's not true of all animals. A few *can* grow new limbs. If a salamander loses a leg, it can grow a new one.

So if a salamander can grow a new leg, why can't we?

Perhaps one day we *will* be able to—with the help of science.

Scientists have recently found a way of changing the cells in a chick so that the chick can grow a new wing if its wing is removed. And if a chick can be made so that it can grow a new wing, then perhaps a human that can grow a new leg could be created, too.

WHY DO MY FEET STINK?

Maybe you, like me, sometimes have stinky feet. Why *do* our feet get stinky? Well, it's all because of those tiny living creatures called *bacteria*. Your feet sweat. Sweat doesn't stink. But the bacteria living on your feet and in your shoes and socks like to live in a dark, warm, moist place—like inside your sweaty shoe—and those bacteria break down your sweat to make some pretty bad-smelling substances.

Smelly feet gross out other people. But not everything hates stinky feet. In fact, mosquitoes love them.

Recently, scientists discovered that mosquitoes love, and fly toward, stinky, three-day-old socks. They also love certain types of stinky cheese. That's because the same bacteria that make your feet stink also live in that stinky cheese. So it's not surprising stinky feet smell like stinky cheese!

"I like the way my own feet smell. I love to smell my sneakers when I take them off."

Christina Ricci (born 1980)
Actress

WHY DO I HAVE A BELLY-BUTTON?

Your bellybutton is what's left of your *umbilical cord* after it was cut. When you were growing inside your mother's womb, you were connected to her by a cord—an umbilical cord. Down this cord came everything you needed in order to stay alive and grow—oxygen, water, and food.

Of course, once you popped out, you didn't need your umbilical cord any more. You could now breathe air with your lungs and take in milk through your mouth. So the cord was cut. Your bellybutton is the nub left where the cord came out of your belly.

People who believe that God created the first human being—Adam—have sometimes wondered whether or not Adam had a bellybutton. After all, if God made Adam, then he was never in a womb and so he wouldn't have a bellybutton. However, Adam is usually shown in art with a bellybutton. I guess it would look strange if he didn't have one.

WHY DO I NEED SLEEP?

Why do we need sleep? Almost every kind of animal sleeps. Cats sleep. Dogs sleep. Birds sleep. Even some fish go into a sort of rest state a little like sleep. But *why*?

One theory says that when we sleep, our bodies can be repaired. But why can't they be repaired while we're awake? Another theory says we sleep to save energy.

However, the truth is, we don't really know why we sleep. Despite the fact that we spend a lot of our lives sleeping, we still don't really understand why we do it! It's a scientific mystery still to be solved.

Why do you think you need sleep? Perhaps, if you become a scientist, you will be able to solve this puzzle.

COULD I LIVE FOREVER?

As the years pass, we get older. But do we *have* to age or die? Why couldn't we stay as fit and healthy as we are at 20 for hundreds, or thousands, of years?

In the story *The Picture of Dorian Gray*, Dorian has a magical portrait of himself. In the picture Dorian gets older, but he himself stays young. It is only when the portrait is destroyed that Dorian instantly ages and dies.

Would you want to stay young for many, many years, like Dorian? Would you want to live forever?

We aren't able to live forever. But perhaps, with the help of science, we will be able to live much longer. Scientists have already discovered that some of our aging seems to be built into us. We are programmed by our *genes*—the blueprints for making our bodies that are stored inside of each human cell—to age and eventually die. Perhaps, one day, science will be able to change our genes, so we don't age as fast.

But would this be a good thing? One problem that it might create is overcrowding. There are already too many human beings on our planet. If people started living a lot longer, there would be a great many more!

"The tragedy of old age is not that one is old, but that one is young."

Lord Henry Wotton
From *The Picture of Dorian Gray* (1890)
by Oscar Wilde

WHY DO I CATCH COLDS?

People get sick for all types of reasons. One common cause of illness is the *virus*. Viruses are incredibly tiny biological objects. Most are so small, they can't be seen down a normal microscope. Instead, they have to be looked at using a more powerful piece of equipment called an *electron microscope*.

Some viruses can get inside our bodies and make us sick. One virus that has almost certainly invaded your own body at some point is the cold virus. How does the virus get inside of you? How do you catch a cold?

Someone with a cold might sneeze, spraying the cold virus into the air, and you might breathe some of it in. Or, you might first touch a doorknob that someone with the virus has used and then touch the food you are eating.

Once the virus gets inside your body, it finds its way inside some of the cells in your nose and throat. It then uses your own cells to start reproducing itself, which starts to make you sick.

Luckily, your body has a defense mechanism against the cold virus. It makes and sends out proteins called *antibodies* to seek out and attack the virus. Special cells in your body then destroy infected cells to finish off the virus. That's the end of your cold. But it takes a few days for the immune system to do the job.

Many serious illnesses are caused by viruses, including measles, polio, chickenpox, and influenza ("flu"). The flu virus is always changing, and new versions occasionally appear and sweep the world, killing millions of people.

What can we do to prevent viruses from spreading? Wash hands regularly and cover our mouths when we sneeze.

We can also protect ourselves by being *immunized*. You've almost certainly had injections to protect you against serious diseases such as polio. The injection contains a little bit of a dead or weakened virus. Your body then learns to make antibodies that will kill the virus. The cells containing these antibodies stand guard in your body, like ninjas, to protect you against a future invasion.

WHY DO I FEEL PAIN?

You feel pain for a reason. Pain is a warning—it tells you that there's something wrong with your body that needs to be fixed and prevents you from repeating an action that is causing pain. Pain tells you when you've twisted your ankle, for example. This makes you stop running and prevents further damage. So, yes, pain isn't a nice experience, but it is a good thing!

A very few people cannot feel pain *at all.* They don't have the type of nerves in their body that cause pain. This can be dangerous, especially when they are young, because they don't know when they have injured themselves. So you should be grateful if you are able to feel pain!

HOW DOES A MEDICINE MAKE ME BETTER?

There are many kinds of medicines, and they work in many different ways. Among the most widely used types of medicines are antibiotics such as penicillin.

In 1928, a scientist named Alexander Fleming was growing bacteria in a dish to use in an experiment. Fleming noticed that a mold had started growing in the dish. He was about to throw it away, when he saw that, amazingly, a substance in the mold was killing the bacteria. Fleming called this substance *penicillin*.

When scientists later gave penicillin to patients with bacterial infections, they got better!

Today, if you get a nasty infection, such as blood poisoning or pneumonia, your doctor will probably give you penicillin to kill off the bacteria.

WHY AM I LUCKY?

One reason you're lucky is that, unlike almost all of the previous generations of children that have been born over hundreds of thousands of years, you have a very good chance of becoming a grownup.

For much of human history, about a third to a half of each generation of children has died. Many were killed by infections and diseases that we have only very recently learned how to prevent.

Perhaps you can think of other reasons why you are lucky?

HOW DO WE KNOW A MEDICINE WORKS?

Medicine didn't always work as well as it does now. For around 2,000 years, until the late 1800s, people treated illnesses by *bloodletting*. Patients' veins and arteries were cut open to let out the "bad" blood.

Now we know that taking lots of blood out of a sick person doesn't really help them get better. So why *did* people believe bloodletting made them better?

Well, sometimes when people were bled, they got better. When that happened, the doctors thought that it was due to the bloodletting. But actually, people often get better anyway, don't they? So how can we be sure that a medicine really works?

We have to do an experiment. We need to divide a group of people randomly into two groups and just give one group the medicine. If the group that had the medicine gets better, and the other (known as the *control group*) doesn't, that's evidence that the medicine works.

Or *is* it? Actually, if you tell people that they are being given medicine, many will *believe* that it works and will say that it works, even if it doesn't! This is called the *placebo effect*.

A famous case was reported by Dr. Henry Beecher during World War Two. Beecher was treating injured soldiers, when he ran out of the pain-killing drug morphine. So he gave them a harmless liquid instead, but *told* them it was morphine. Amazingly, the *fake* medicine seemed to work—the soldiers said that their pain was reduced!

To be sure that our medicine *really* works then, we should probably not tell either group whether they are getting real or fake medicine. And maybe the doctors giving the medicine shouldn't know, either.

If most people in the group that got the real medicine get better, but the control group doesn't, that would be fairly good evidence that our medicine really works.

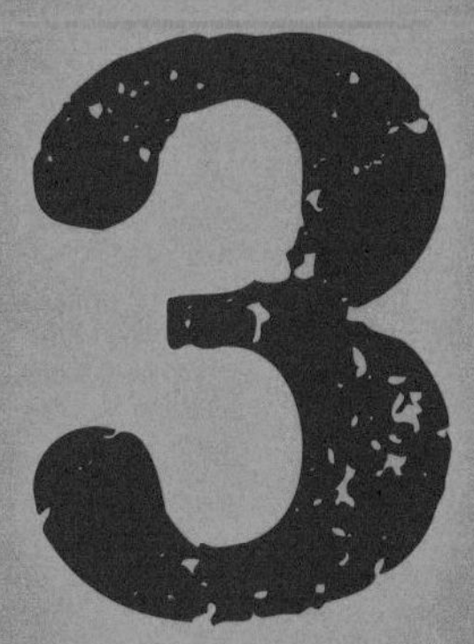

MIND-BOGGLING ME

Unlike bricks, grass, volcanoes, and planets, we human beings have minds. Our minds are extraordinary. In fact, they are one of the wonders of the cosmos. On this tiny planet, lost in this huge and ancient physical universe, minds have appeared!

Of course, it's not just humans that have minds. Other animals have them, too. But humans have minds that are particularly special. One reason they are special is that we can think deeply about who and what we are and where we came from. We can also think about morality—about what's right and what's wrong. And we have a very powerful and much more complex language than other animals. By just making a few sounds—or putting a few squiggles on a sheet of paper—I can transmit my thoughts to others. In fact, I am doing it right now . . .

WHAT IS MY MIND?

You have a *mind*, but what does that mean?

Well, for a start, it means that you have *experiences*. Right now you are experiencing this book. You can *see* the paper, *feel* it with your fingers, and *hear* it rustle as you turn the pages. You could also *smell* and *taste* it if you wanted to (though I wouldn't recommend that!). You have other types of experiences, too—*pain*, for example, and also *emotions* such as happiness and sadness.

You can also *do things* with your mind. You are able to *think* and *figure things out*—like the solution to a puzzle. You can also *remember things* that have happened to you, *make plans* for the future, and *understand* language—including the words that you are reading right now!

WHERE IS MY MIND?

So, now you know *what* your mind is. But *where* is it?

Is it your brain?

Your brain is a gray, walnut-shaped organ hidden away inside your skull—about the size of both of your fists stuck together.

Many brain scientists believe that your mind and brain are exactly the same thing, and almost everyone agrees that, at the very least, your mind and brain affect each other.

What goes on in your brain *has been shown to affect your mind*—by stimulating your brain with electricity, scientists can make you laugh, cry, or experience a certain memory. Give your brain a bang and that can affect your mind by knocking you unconscious. Drugs can also affect how we feel by changing what's happening in our brains. For example, some chemicals can make us feel happier.

We also know that damage to our brain can affect our minds. In 1848, a man named Phineas Gage accidentally got an iron rod stuck through his head. Phineas survived, but his personality changed a lot.

Scientists have also discovered that what goes on in your mind *affects what happens in your brain*. Even if your mind isn't your brain, it certainly affects what goes on in there. When you decide to move your arm, something happens in your brain that causes an electrical signal to run down the nerves in your arm. That moves your muscles, which then move your arm. And using MRI scanners, scientists can see, for example, that when people relax and meditate, what's happening in their brain changes, too.

People haven't always known that our minds and brains affect each other. Some ancient Greeks thought that our heart was where we did all our thinking, while the brain was just an organ for cooling the blood.

So your mind and brain do affect each other. But are they actually the *same thing*?

Perhaps your experiences, thoughts, and memories are just things going on *in your brain*? Might a feeling of happiness, say, be *just* something happening in your brain? If so, then your mind is located where your brain is—in your head, between your ears.

However, not everyone believes that they are the same thing. Some think that our experiences and thoughts are something more than what's going on physically in our brains.

But if your mind is *not* your brain, *what* is it and *where* is it? These aren't easy questions to answer!

COULD I HAVE A PAIN IN THIN AIR?

Sometimes, after someone has had a leg removed, they still feel a pain where their leg used to be. It's a very strange experience for them, of course. Ask them where the pain seems to be, and they point into *thin air*.

So where is their pain? It can't be in their leg, as that is no longer there. So *where is it, then*? Is it in their leg stump, perhaps? Or in their brain? Philosophers and scientists disagree about where such "phantom" pains are really located. What do you think?

"Pain is temporary. Quitting lasts forever."

Lance Armstrong (born 1971)
Former professional cyclist

COULD I FEEL YOUR PAIN?

Minds appear to be hidden in a strange way. Your brain, of course, is hidden from other people—it's inside of your skull. But at least it is *possible* for others to *see* it. If a window were put in your skull, people could peek inside and see your brain. Scientists can also use a brain scanner to reveal what's going on inside of it.

So your brain is hidden, but it can be observed by others. What about your mind? Two people might have very similar, or even exactly the same, experiences, of course. You and I might both fall over and tell each other we have pain in our knees. But it seems that our pain is separate—there are two pains because there are two of *us*. I can't experience your pain—only mine. I can never get inside your mind to find out what your experience is like, to feel your pain along with you.

Although scientists can *observe* what's happening in your brain when you're in pain, it seems that no one else can ever feel your pain. It seems your pains and other experiences are hidden in a way that what happens in your brain is not.

Does that show that your experiences are not just what happens in your brain? What do you think?

HOW DOES MY BRAIN WORK?

Human brains are complicated things. They are largely made up of tiny cells called *neurons*. There are about 80 to 100 billion (100,000,000,000) neurons in our brains. That's about the same as the number of *trees* in the Amazon rainforest!

These cells form a complex web, pulsing with electrical activity. The number of connections in this web is similar to the amount of *leaves* in the Amazon rainforest.

Your brain is plugged into your nervous system—the system of nerves linking your brain to the rest of your body. Your brain sends out electrical signals to move muscles, pump blood, keep you breathing, and control the substances produced by your glands. Your brain also receives patterns of electrical signals from your body, such as those sent by your fingertips, eyes, ears, nose, and mouth.

So your brain is a type of central control room that monitors and is in charge of what's going on in your body.

Other creatures have brains, but some have only very simple ones. The brain of a fruit fly has 100,000 neurons (you have a million times as many as that). The brain of a nematode worm has only 302 neurons. And some, such as starfish and jellyfish, have *no* brain at all!

ARE MY THOUGHTS IN MY BRAIN?

Suppose you have a thought—"I want some cheese!" That leads you to act—you go to the fridge to get some cheese.

Most scientists will say that your actions—the movement to the fridge, opening the door, getting the cheese—happen because of a chain of *earlier* physical causes. Your legs walk because your muscles move. Your muscles move because of electrical signals from your brain.

Things that happen *in* your brain have physical causes, too—what happens in one part may be caused by what happens in another part. Brain events are also caused by physical stimulation from outside of your brain—produced by your eyes, ears, nose, and so on.

Now of course *if* your mind *is* your brain, then your mind is part of this chain of physical causes—it can cause you to open the fridge. But if your mind *isn't* something physical—suppose it's something extra—then it seems that *it couldn't have any effect on what your body does*!

After all, if your mind isn't physical, your legs would *still* take you to the fridge—even if you decided *not* to! Your legs would still be caused to move by what's going on physically inside of your brain.

It seems that the only way your mind can affect your body, is if it is *itself* physical!

This has led many people to believe that *you are your brain*, and that there's nothing more to the mind than the brain and what goes on in it. True, your thoughts and feelings don't *seem* like something that's happening in your brain. But then how things *seem* isn't always how things *are*.

Do you think your thoughts are in your brain, or do you think they are somewhere else?

HOW DO I KNOW OTHER

Take a look at the people around you. You suppose they have minds, of course. But do you *know* they have minds?

After all, it seems that minds can't be seen. Your mind is a place to which only you have access. It's like a secret garden—a garden filled, not with trees and flowers, but with thoughts and feelings. And it's a garden that you alone can enter. Others can never get inside your mind. And you cannot enter their minds, either. All you can *directly* observe of other human beings is their physical bodies and how they behave.

True, other human beings behave much like you do. Just like you, they jump up and down and shout "Ow!" when they stub their toe. They too claim to feel happy or sad. Just like you, they *say* they have minds. So isn't this good evidence that they feel pain, too?

Maybe not. Imagine you wandered into a strange and magical landscape—very different to our actual world. You wander up to a flower and peek inside. There, hidden inside the flower, is a fairy. Are you justified in thinking that *every* flower in that world has a fairy inside? Of course not! Just because *one* flower has a fairy in it, that doesn't give you much reason to believe that the other flowers have fairies in them, too.

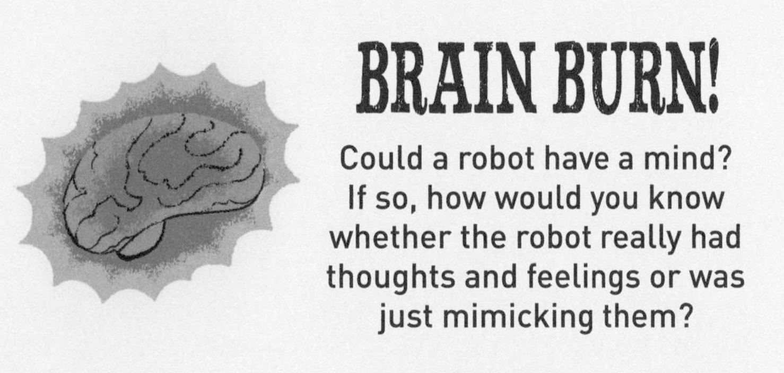

BRAIN BURN!

Could a robot have a mind? If so, how would you know whether the robot really had thoughts and feelings or was just mimicking them?

PEOPLE HAVE MINDS?

Now think about humans and their minds. The only human whose mind you can observe is *you*. You know that behind your *own* behavior there's a mind. But that doesn't give you much reason to suppose that behind the behavior of other humans lie other minds, does it? To suppose this would be like concluding that most or all flowers contain fairies when you have only seen inside one. And that conclusion isn't justified at all!

So how *do* you know that other people have minds as well as bodies? How do you know that they aren't just mindless robots or flesh-and-blood machines?

How do you know that yours isn't *the only mind there is*?

This is a very famous philosophical puzzle called the *problem of other minds*. There's no agreement about how to solve it. Can you figure out a solution?

CAN I MOVE THINGS WITH MY MIND?

Some people believe that people can move things using only their minds. Just by thinking. This ability is called *telekinesis*. Some people claim that they can make pencils roll or levitate small objects—make them float in midair. Others claim they can even levitate themselves!

However, creating the illusion they can do these things is something that many conjurers have mastered. There are all kinds of tricks they use to fool people into *thinking* that they have the power of telekinesis.

In the 1980s, the McDonnell Laboratory for Psychical Research claimed that two subjects had actually been able to bend metal and cause images to appear on film by the power of their minds. In truth, the two men were conjurers who wanted to show that even trained scientists could be fooled.

Most scientists agree that no one has *ever* been able to demonstrate that they have any real telekinetic power. While it would be exciting to believe that we have such powers, it has to be said that we probably don't!

WHY DO I SEE FACES EVERYWHERE?

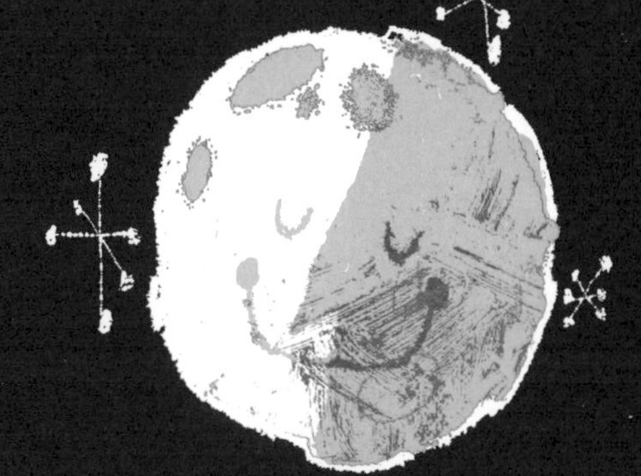

I'm sure you have stared up at clouds, or looked into the dying embers of a fire, and seen all kinds of things. Often, we see faces.

Why *do* we see faces so easily?

Part of the reason is that we rely on our ability to spot and understand faces. So we have evolved to be sensitive to them. In fact, we're so sensitive that we can often "see" a face even when there isn't actually one there.

Another reason why we can often find faces in the embers of a fire or passing clouds is that occasionally, by chance, these patterns will look like faces *anyway*.

Put these two factors together, and the illusory face that they create can be dramatic! A famous example is the *Face on Mars*. On July 25, 1976, a probe called *Viking 1* was taking pictures of Mars. One picture caused enormous interest. There, on the surface of the planet, appeared to be a huge face.

But, as you have probably guessed, the *Face on Mars* was no such thing. Later photographs revealed that the face was really just a hill that looked nothing like a face, except when lit at a certain angle so that the shadows happened to fall in a way that made it look facelike.

The *Face on Mars* was a result of two things: a coincidence—that shadows looked facelike—and our ability to *see* a face even when there isn't one.

Every year, miraculous appearances of faces are reported on the backs of doors, burned on to pieces of toast, in halves of fruit, and so on. Many are thought to be the faces of religious figures, such as Jesus.

But are they really?

4

WHAT CAN I KNOW?

Humans don't know everything, but we do think that we know a lot about the universe we live in. Scientists have discovered all types of facts about the universe, such as how old our planet is and that it moves. And of course, you can know things by observing the world around you. You know that you live in a world containing mountains and seas, plants and animals. And you know that you are looking at a book right now.

So you and I know quite a bit. *Or do we?*

There are some famous philosophical puzzles about how much, if anything, we can know about the universe. These puzzles seem to show that, actually, you can't know very much, perhaps even nothing at all, about the world around you.

In this chapter, we'll look at two of these puzzles. I'll let you make up your own mind about whether they can be solved.

HOW DO I KNOW THAT I'M NOT DREAMING?

Have you ever had a dream in which you thought that you were awake? I have. In fact, sometimes I have been convinced that I've woken up but then discovered I was still dreaming!

So how can I be sure that I am not dreaming right now? How can you? Maybe you are tucked in bed, fast asleep. How can you tell that you're not?

It's true that peculiar things sometimes happen in dreams—I've dreamed that I can fly, for example. I know that's impossible, so if I discover I can fly, that's a good clue that I'm dreaming.

But even if we can sometimes tell that we are dreaming, how can you tell right now that we're not? Maybe you are having a vivid and realistic dream at this very moment, and this book is part of your dream!

Do you think you can tell that you're not dreaming? Can you tell by pinching yourself? Or in some other way?

HOW DO I KNOW THAT THE WORLD IS REAL?

What if our world was an elaborate illusion created by someone or something else?

French philosopher René Descartes tried to question everything. One day, when he was sitting beside a fire, he wondered if he might be the victim of a deceiving demon. Descartes thought that perhaps a demon was creating an illusion in Descartes's mind that he was sitting beside the fire. He then wondered whether *everything* he had ever experienced was an illusion conjured up by a demon.

This idea about deceiving demons is certainly disturbing. It challenges our assumption that we know a lot about our world. If everything could seem exactly the same to us, and yet could be an illusion, how can we know that it's real?

Do we have no more reason to think that this world is real than we have to think that's it's an illusion? Some philosophers think that we *can't* know anything about the world; others think that we *can*. Some say that it's reasonable to believe the simplest explanation of what we experience—it's much simpler to believe how things *seem* is how they *are*, rather than that there's a demon conjuring up an illusion.

"What if you were unable to wake from that dream, Neo? How would you know the difference between the dream world and the real world?"

Morpheus
From the movie *The Matrix* (1999)

HOW DO I KNOW I AM REAL?

How can you be sure that you exist? Maybe you are just a figment of someone's imagination! Could *you* be an illusion?

Descartes thought that if you are thinking—if you are questioning things—then you must exist. He thought that you might be wrong about many things, but you can't be wrong about the fact that you exist. His statement: *I think, therefore I am* was his proof that he really existed.

Does Descartes's proof work? Couldn't an evil demon cause us to make mistakes in even our simplest proofs—including this one? Perhaps the demon has made Descartes's reasoning go wrong, even here?

HOW DO I KNOW THAT THE SUN WILL RISE TOMOROW?

Let's look at a puzzle that questions our knowledge of all of those parts of the universe that we haven't observed yet. Most of the universe lies beyond what we have directly experienced. No one has experienced the future, because it hasn't arrived yet. Nor can we observe what Earth was like millions of years ago or see what lies at the center of Earth.

Yet we believe that we know a lot about our universe. For example, we are pretty sure that the middle of Earth is made of molten iron, and not molten cheese.

We also think that we know what will happen tomorrow: that the sun will rise, for example. Of course, we realize that we could be mistaken. After all, a comet might crash into Earth tonight and stop it from spinning on its axis. In which case, the sun won't rise above the horizon tomorrow. That's a possibility—but it's not a very *likely* possibility. So we suppose we are justified in believing that the sun will rise tomorrow.

Why is this? Well—it's because we have seen it rise in the past. I saw it rise every day this year, so I think it will rise tomorrow because of past experience.

But, when we reason in this way, aren't we assuming that the universe is regular? What I mean is, aren't we assuming that what happens in one place tends to happen in other places, and that what happens at one time tends to happen at other times? But maybe the universe isn't like that.

Maybe, rather than having a regular pattern, the universe is like a patchwork quilt, with little fragments of pattern, but no overall pattern. Maybe, tomorrow, like ants crawling across a patchwork quilt, we'll arrive at a different bit of pattern and everything will behave differently. Perhaps the sun won't rise, and an enormous sunflower will appear instead.

If we could justify our belief that there *is* a regular pattern to the universe, then we could justify our belief that the sun will rise tomorrow, because that's what has happened in the past. But how can we *know* that the universe does have a regular pattern? Not by looking at what it's like here at the moment and then concluding it must be like that everywhere else. Such an argument would just *assume* the universe has a regular pattern!

So what reason do we have to believe that nature is regular? If we don't have any, then it seems not just that we can't be *sure* that the sun will rise tomorrow, we actually have no reason at all to suppose that it will. It's just as reasonable to think that an enormous sunflower will rise instead!

That conclusion seems crazy, of course. But is it *true*? Philosophers are still arguing about that. What do you think—can we *know* that the sun will rise tomorrow?

WHAT SHOULD I

There are so many different things you might believe, of course. And most of them aren't true. For example, you might believe that the Arctic is populated with giant ant people and that sneezing makes your head explode.

Does it matter if we believe what isn't true? Well, it certainly matters if I believe that drinking toilet cleaner is good for me or that I can breathe underwater. False beliefs can hurt us.

So, if we want to believe what's true, what is the best way of making sure that most of our beliefs are true?

Applying your powers of reason is a very good method. Try thinking like a detective. When detectives have a difficult murder case to solve, they carefully weigh up the evidence. They carefully construct and check their arguments. Detectives can't always figure out who did it, of course. And sometimes they get things wrong.

BELIEVE?

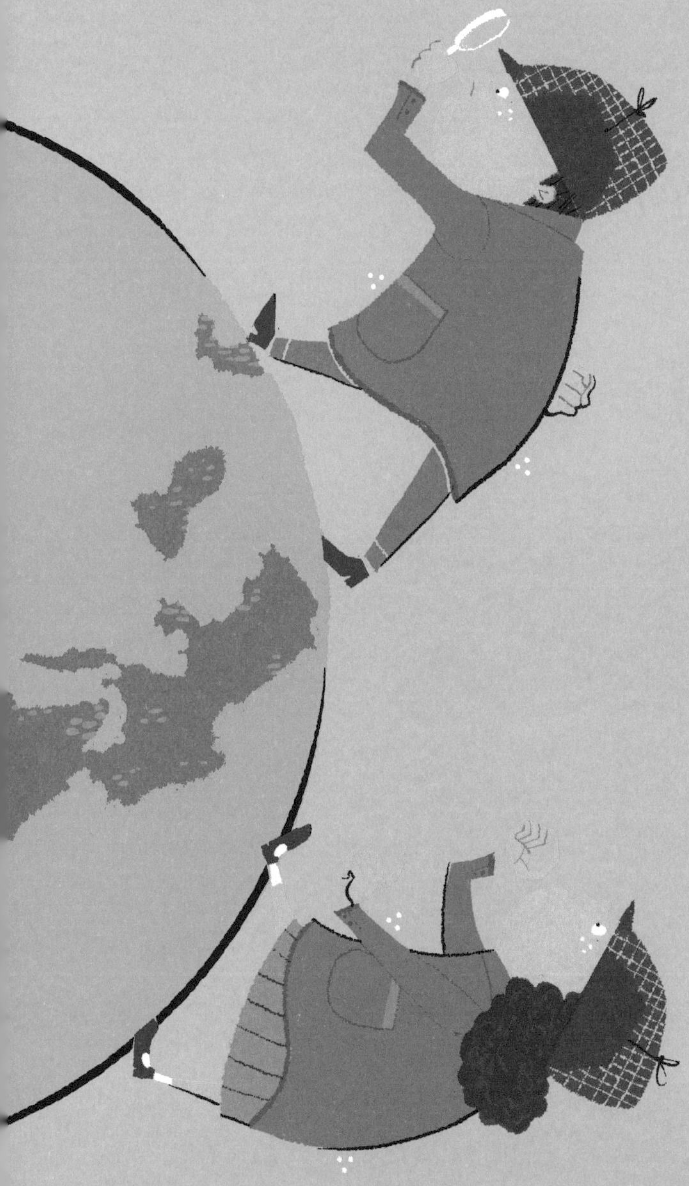

However, applying reason is certainly a much better way of deciding who's guilty than randomly sticking a pin in a list of names or tossing a coin.

Think of your head as a basket toward which all types of beliefs are tumbling. Some of them are true, but many are false. You need some sort of filter that will let in true beliefs but keep out false ones. Your head will soon fill up with nonsense otherwise.

Your ability to question and reason may not be a perfect filter—but it's pretty good. So make sure that you don't turn off your reasoning skills!

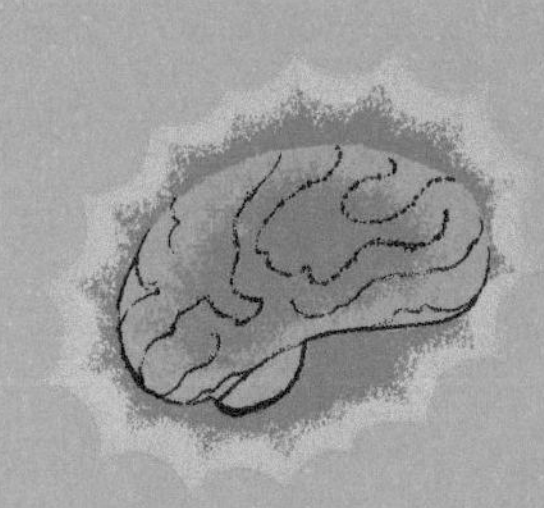

BRAIN BURN!

Is it sometimes better to believe things that aren't true? If so, when and why?

GLOSSARY

Words in **bold** refer to other glossary entries.

AFTERLIFE Refers to life after death. Some religious people believe that we go to heaven when we die. Others believe that we are **reincarnated**—reborn into new bodies such as a human, a wasp, or even a plant.

ANCIENT GREEKS People who lived in Greece around 2,500 years ago.

ANTIBODIES Tiny, ninjalike things formed by your body as part of its immune system. Antibodies find and help destroy invading bodies such as **bacteria** and **viruses**.

ATOMS Tiny particles of an element, from which all **physical** objects are made. Atoms themselves have parts, including **electrons**, **neutrons**, and protons.

BACTERIA Microscopic single-celled organisms found almost everywhere on the surface of Earth. They are also called microbes or germs. Some types of bacteria can cause infections, but others, such as those living in your intestines, are good for you.

BILLION One thousand million (or 1,000,000,000).

BLIND SPOT The small area at the back of the eye where there are no light-sensitive **cells**. This causes a section in your field of vision where you are blind—although you don't normally notice it.

BRAIN The big, walnut-shaped, gray-colored **organ** inside of your **skull**.

CELLS The basic building blocks of life. All living things are cells or are built out of cells.

COMET An icy ball that circles the Sun. When comets are close to the Sun, they have tails.

DECEIVE To deceive someone is to trick them into believing something that is not true. Lying is one way of deceiving someone.

DESCARTES, RENÉ (1596–1650) A famous French **philosopher**. *The Meditations of First Philosophy* is his best-known book.

ELECTRON MICROSCOPE Microscopes are used to observe very small objects. An electron microscope uses a beam of tiny particles called **electrons** instead of light to illuminate the object. Electron microscopes are much more powerful than microscopes that use light.

ELECTRONS Very tiny, negatively charged particles that form part of an **atom**.

ELEMENTS Substances made from just one kind of **atom**. There are 118 known elements, including carbon and hydrogen.

ENERGY The **physical** power to do something. Power plants produce electrical energy to power our TVs and refrigerators, for example.

EXPERIENCE We experience the world around us using our senses of touch, taste, hearing, sight, and smell. We also experience emotions, such as happiness and fear, and sensations such as pain. There may be other kinds of experiences, too, such as religious experiences.

FAMILY TREE The relationships within a family throughout **generations**, for example, your mother, father, grandparents, and great-grandparents.

FERTILIZE New animals produced through sexual reproduction begin when an egg is fertilized by a sperm. This is a key part of how animals **reproduce**.

GALVANI, LUIGI (1737–1798) An Italian physicist and physician.

GENERATION You are part of a generation of human beings—your mother and father are the preceding generation. They are preceded by your grandparents' generation, and so on.

GENES Chemical instructions made of DNA that can be found in the nucleus of a **cell**. Genes contain the information needed to build a human body and also information on how to build and maintain your cells.

GLAND An organ in the body that produces chemical substances that the body needs in order to work properly.

HYPOTHESIS A claim about the world—based on something we have not actually observed. For example, if you see a pair of shoes sticking out from under a curtain, you might form the hypothesis that there is someone behind the curtain (though the shoes could be empty, of course). You could test your hypothesis by pulling back the curtain or feeling through the curtain.

ILLUSION Something that we observe that is misleading.

LENS Part of the eye that focuses light from an object onto the **retina** to form an image. The lens is behind the **pupil**.

LOCKE, JOHN (1632–1704) An important English **philosopher**.

MEDITATE People usually meditate by trying to empty their mind of all thoughts or by focusing intently on something. This may help people feel calm and tranquil. Many religious traditions include forms of meditation.

MOLECULE A tiny bundle of two or more **atoms** bound together.

MRI SCANNER A scanner that uses powerful magnets and radio waves to reveal what's inside a **physical** object, such as a human body.

MUSCLES Muscles are a type of tissue, and they help support our skeletons and move our bodies. Muscles are joined to bones by **tendons**.

NERVES Nerves are cablelike structures used to transmit electrical impulses around the body.

NERVOUS SYSTEM The network of **nerve cells** and fibers that transmits electrical impulses around the body in order to control its vital functions such as breathing. It is made up of the **brain**, spinal cord, and nerves.

NEURON A special type of **cell** that can transmit a small electrical impulse to neighboring neurons; a **nerve** cell.

NUTRIENTS The substances needed for a living thing to live and grow.

OPTIC NERVE The **nerve** that transmits impulses from the **retina** to the **brain**.

ORGAN A part of the body with a special function. For example, the heart is an organ used to pump blood.

PHILOSOPHER A thinker who addresses some of the biggest questions of all (they are usually questions that don't appear to be answerable by the **scientific method**).

PHYSICAL The physical **universe** is the universe of physical matter and **energy** existing in time and space. But is the physical universe all there is?

PLACEBO A fake treatment or medicine. Although if the patient believes it is real, it may actually have a positive effect.

PROBE A device used to find things out. Space probes are unmanned spacecraft that are sent into space to find out about our solar system and beyond.

PROOF Evidence that something is true or a fact.

PUPIL The hole in the center of the iris that allows light to enter the eye.

REINCARNATION A form of **afterlife**. Some people believe that after you die, you are reborn, although not necessarily as a human being.

RELATIVES Members of your family, for example, your mother and father, brothers and sisters, grandparents, and everyone else who forms part of your **family tree**.

REPRODUCE Living things can reproduce, which means to create new individuals.

RETINA The surface at the back of the eye that contains light-sensitive **cells**, called rods and cones. These cells change light into **nerve** impulses that are sent to the **brain** so it can figure out what the eye is seeing.

SCIENTIFIC METHOD A special way of trying to find things out. The scientific method is based on observation, measurement, and experiment. **Scientists** develop **theories** or **hypotheses** about the world, which they test and then modify where necessary.

SCIENTIST A person who tries to find things out using the **scientific method**.

SKULL The hard bone around your head that protects your **brain**.

SPECIES A group of animals or plants that can breed together and produce offspring. Humans are a species.

TENDON A long, tough cord of tissue that joins **muscle** to bone. There is a noticeable tendon at the back of your foot that connects your heel bone to your calf muscle. It is called the Achilles tendon. You can also see tendons on the backs of your hands and below your wrists.

THEORY An idea about how or why something happens.

TRILLION A million million (or 1,000,000,000,000).

UNCONSCIOUS A condition in which a person is unaware of their surroundings and cannot see, feel, or think.

UNIVERSE All of space and everything that exists in it. It includes our solar system and the **billions** of stars and planets beyond it. Some **scientists** believe that our **universe** is not the only one.

VIRUS A tiny infectious agent that can only **reproduce** itself inside of other living organisms. The cold virus, for example, infects and lives inside human beings, where it reproduces itself. Then we sneeze and pass it on to someone else.

VISUAL CORTEX The part of the **brain** that deals with sight. It is at the back of your brain and is connected to your eyes by the **optic nerve**.

INDEX

FURTHER READING

BOOKS

Philosophy for Kids: 40 Fun Questions That Help You Wonder . . . About Everything!—David White
The Complete Philosophy Files—Stephen Law
Who Am I?—Richard Walker
Why Eating Bogeys Is Good for You—Mitchell Symons
Why Is Snot Green?—Glenn Murphy

WEBSITES

Human body:
http://kidshealth.org/kid

Optical illusions:
http://kids.niehs.nih.gov/games/illusions/index.htm

The Science Museum's *Who Am I?* site:
www.sciencemuseum.org.uk/WhoAmI

CHALLENGE YOUR THINKING

Finding things out about the world, and ourselves, can be tricky. Here is a famous example showing a mistake that people often make:

Imagine I show you a small target that I have hit with ten bullets from 165 ft. (50m) away. Impressed by my skill? Am I an expert marksman?

Are you sure?

To be certain that I am an expert marksman, you need to count *not just my hits, but also my misses*. If you had looked at the wall behind the target, you would have seen that it's covered with thousands of holes—my misses! This shows that actually I am a terrible shot—I just got lucky ten times.

So remember—don't just look for things that support what you believe. Also look for evidence that might show that you're wrong. *Put what you believe to the test!* The very best thinkers are those who can spot their mistakes and learn from them.